# SCIENCE FRONTIERS

# GREEN POWER

## ECO-ENERGY WITHOUT POLLUTION

### DAVID JEFFERIS

## Crabtree Publishing Company

www.crabtreebooks.com

# INTRODUCTION

**O**ur energy needs used to be met almost entirely by burning **fossil fuels**, such as coal, oil, or gas. Oil and gas are non-**renewable** resources, which means they will one day run out, probably within the next 100 years.

Until the mid-1900s, few people worried about **pollution** or fuel supply shortages. Today, the pollution created by burning fossil fuels is seen as a health hazard. The waste gases from fossil fuels also change Earth's climate.

Many alternative energy sources that are renewable and do not harm the environment are now being developed.

Crabtree Publishing Company
www.crabtreebooks.com

PMB 16A
350 Fifth Ave.
Ste. 3308
New York
NY 10118

616 Welland Ave
St. Catharines, ON
Canada
L2M 5V6

**Edited by**
Isabella McIntyre

**Coordinating editor**
Ellen Rodger

**Project editors**
Carrie Gleason
L. Michelle Nielsen

**Production Coordinator**
Rosie Gowsell

**Educational advisor**
Julie Stapleton

**Technical consultant**
Mat Irvine FBIS

**Created and produced by**
David Jefferis/BuzzBooks

©2006 David Jefferis/BuzzBooks

**Cataloging-in-Publication Data**
Jefferis, David.
  Green power : eco-energy without
pollution / written by David Jefferis.
    p. cm. -- (Science frontiers)
  Includes bibliographical references
and index.
    ISBN-13: 978-0-7787-2857-3 (rlb)
    ISBN-10: 0-7787-2857-9 (rlb)
    ISBN-13: 978-0-7787-2871-9 (pbk)
    ISBN-10: 0-7787-2871-4 (pbk)

1. Energy development--Environmental
aspects--Juvenile literature. 2.
Renewable energy sources--Juvenile
literature.  I. Title.

TD195.E49J44 2006
333.79--dc22

2005035762
LC

Pictures on these pages, clockwise
from above left:

1 SunDiesel is a clean biofuel made
from woodchips.
2 Electricity moves to homes and
businesses along power lines
like these.
3 Huge wind turbines are being built
all over the world.
4 This newly designed car runs on
electric power from a hydrogen fuel
cell.

# CONTENTS

# WHAT IS GREEN POWER?

**G**reen power describes the kinds of energy that create little or no pollution. Green power fuels are renewable, which means they are replaced as they are used, unlike oil or gas.

▲ Vehicle engines run cleaner today than in the past. Waste gases from car exhausts are still one of the biggest polluters.

**T**here are three big problems with the non-renewable fossil fuels coal, oil, and gas. One problem is that oil and gas supplies are being used up. Most experts believe that the biggest oil fields and natural gas deposits have already been discovered. As the existing supply of oil and gas gets used, prices will rise and eventually there will not be enough to meet the world's energy needs.

▲ Waste gases from jets create pollution in the atmosphere, or layers of gases that surround the Earth, which traps heat and causes temperatures on Earth to increase.

*The polar ice cap in 1979*

*The polar ice cap in 2003*

► Satellite pictures show that the ice cap at the North Pole is melting. Scientists believe this may be caused by global warming.

► The Earth stays about the same temperature because heat received from the Sun is balanced by heat escaping back into space. Water vapor in the air helps create a natural greenhouse effect by trapping heat near the Earth's surface. Extra, human-made greenhouse gases shift this balance by trapping more heat than is needed.

**P**ollution is another problem. At one time, most of our power came from burning coal, which created a lot of dirty smoke. Today, vehicle exhaust is a main polluter. Cars and trucks run cleaner than in the past but the number of vehicles on the road has increased. Pollution can be harmful to the health of people and animals.

Global warming is the most serious problem. Most experts agree that climate change is partly due to burning fossil fuels, because it creates a gas called carbon dioxide. Too much carbon dioxide traps heat in the Earth's atmosphere. This atmosphere heating is called the greenhouse effect.

▲ Hundreds of off-shore rigs drill for oil and gas in the shallow waters of the world's oceans.

Hundreds of other rigs extract oil on land, where drilling costs are lower.

## WHAT ARE FOSSIL FUELS?

Fossil fuel is the name given to coal, oil, and natural gas, all of which are taken from rocks in the Earth's crust, or top layer. These fuels formed from the remains, or fossils, of animals and plants that died millions of years ago and were slowly buried over time.
   Fossil fuels are widely used for heating, for transportation, and for making electricity in power stations.

Until recently, most fossil fuels have been easy to get and were available in large amounts. With the demand for energy climbing fast, especially from countries with large populations, such as India and China, fossil fuel supplies are likely to run short later this century.

Oil rig

Gas

Oil

Mine shaft

Coal seams

# HYDROELECTRICITY

**H**ydroelectric power uses the energy of moving water to turn giant electricity turbines. Huge dams built to control the water flow can cause environmental issues.

**H**ydroelectric power is a renewable resource that supplies about one-fifth of the world's electricity. Norway uses hydroelectricity for almost all its power. Iceland uses it for more than 80 percent. Canada is the world's biggest hydroelectric producer. The La Grand Complex on the La Grande River in northern Quebec is the world's biggest power **generator**.

Hydroelectricity has some big advantages, especially because there are no expensive mining costs involved. Once built, a hydroelectric power plant is fairly cheap to run and can last a long time. Some hydroelectric plants have lasted more than 100 years.

▲ Hydroelectricity has been around a long time. This power station in Austria was built in 1911, using water piped down from the mountain above.

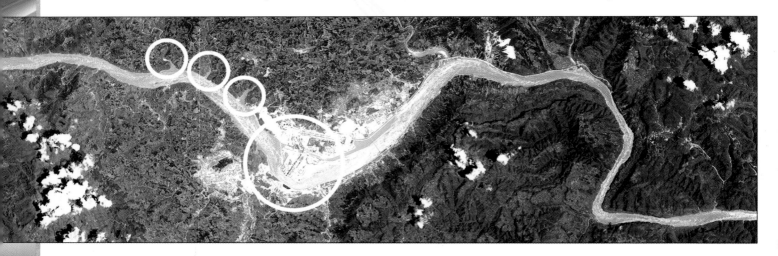

**T**here are also disadvantages to hydroelectric power. Massive dams and generating stations can create environmental problems. Waterways that have been dammed often interupt the migration routes of wild animals. Water gushing below a dam can scour away the river bottom. Plants decay, or rot, in **reservoirs**, which causes another greenhouse gas, methane, to form. A big issue with building a new dam is that large areas of land are flooded by the steadily rising waters of the reservoir. By the time the massive Three Gorges Dam in China is finished in 2009, nearly two million people will have been forced from their homes.

▲ China's Yangtze River is the site of the unfinished Three Gorges Dam (in the big circle). It will be the world's largest dam. The three gorges it is named after (in the small circles) will be flooded.

# ELECTRICITY FROM SPINNING TURBINES

Almost all the electricity we use comes from power stations, using generators based on the experiments of electrical pioneer Michael Faraday, in 1831.

In a hydroelectric power plant, rushing reservoir water provides the force that turns the blades of a turbine. Looking much like a ship's propeller, a turbine can be turned by moving air, steam, or liquid.

The turbine causes magnets to turn past a central wire coil in the generator. This makes electricity.

Electricity output is measured in units called watts (W), named after another early scientist, James Watt. A light bulb is usually 60W to 100W. A family home uses a little more than 1 kilowatt (kW, or 1,000W) for heat, light, television, and other household gadgets.

The Hoover Dam (shown below), one of the biggest power plants in the United States, can produce 2,000 megawatts (mW, or 1,000kW) of electricity. That's enough electricity to light up more than 20 million light bulbs!

Reservoir    Turbine    Generator    Power lines
Dam

◄ The Hoover Dam was the biggest dam in the U.S. when finished in 1936. It is just over 726 feet (221 m) in height and its reservoir, Lake Mead, stretches for 110 miles (177 km) upstream.

▼ A view of the inside of the Hoover Dam's turbine hall (left), and the top of the dam.

# OCEAN POWER

**O**cean energy systems use either the steady but powerful movement of ocean tides or the crashing energy of waves.

**T**he biggest tidal power station is in France, where there is a barrage, or dam, 2,460 feet (750 m) long. The barrage, completed in 1966, crosses the Rance River. There are 24 turbines inside that generate power as tidal waters flow in. At high tide, the closed barrage gates trap the water, forming a big lake upstream. At low tide, the gates open and water flows through the turbines again, and then out to sea.

▲ **The Moon's** gravitational **pull on our planet creates tides. Waves are caused mostly by winds blowing across the sea.**

The Annapolis Tidal Generating Station in Nova Scotia, Canada, was finished in 1984. It produces power for 4,000 homes.

▲ Limpet works like this. Water (1) surges into a concrete chamber (2). Rising water (3) forces air into the upper chamber (4). A rush of air through the tube (5) drives a turbine for electricity.

▲ The Limpet power station in Islay, Scotland, uses waves to create electricity. At night, when demand for electricity is low, Limpet's power is used to recharge an electric bus.

◄ The turbine is bigger than it looks here. Find the life preserver and access door to get a good idea of its true size.

**T**he world's first commercial-scale wave power station is called the Limpet. It was installed in 2000 on the coast of Islay, a small island off Scotland. The Limpet station generates 500 kilowatts of electricity, enough for 300 homes.

Limpet works when crashing waves fill a partly submerged concrete chamber. As the waves churn in, they push a blast of air into a hole, which spins a turbine. As the waves recede, the air is sucked back down into the chamber, spinning the turbine again.

◄ The Rance tidal power station has supplied electricity since it was finished in 1966. Tides in the area are very high, reaching 42 feet (13 meters) or more. There is also a small tidal power station at Kislaya Guba, in Russia.

## UNDERWATER WINDMILL

This underwater windmill is designed to generate power from the steady movement of ocean currents.

It consists of a steel column fixed to the seabed. Mounted to the column are rotor blades, driven by the flow of water in much the same way that windmill sails are turned by the wind.

The main difference between the two is that water is more than 800 times denser than air. This means that slow water speeds are all that is needed to turn the rotor blades. Water flowing past the underwater windmill at a speed of only about six miles per hour (10 km/h) is enough to generate 300 kilowatts of electricity.

The world's first underwater windmill was installed off the coast of England in 2003. In the future, groups of 10 to 20 more machines could easily be placed in the shallow waters.

Maintaining machines at sea is difficult even in good weather. The underwater windmill has a rotor system that slides up to the surface. Repairs are made by technicians aboard ships, instead of by divers.

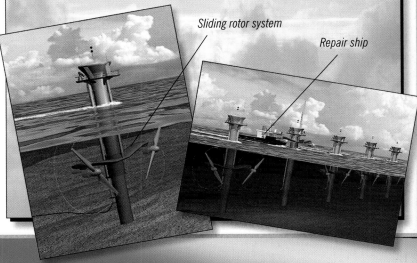

Sliding rotor system

Repair ship

# SOLAR HEATING

**T**he Sun bathes the Earth continuously in heat and light. Each day at dawn, solar power systems start to use this huge source of energy.

▲ This solar furnace was designed by French chemist Antoine Lavoisier (1743-1794) for his experiments. The furnace focused the heat of the Sun using lenses to concentrate the light.

**T**here is no shortage of solar energy. Solar energy comes from our nonstop powerhouse, the Sun. In less than one hour, more solar energy reaches the Earth than is used by the world's entire population in one year.

Amazingly, we harness, or use, less than one percent of this resource. Machines that use the Sun for heating are not new, but efficient designs have only recently been made.

▲ We are about 93 million miles (150 million km) from the Sun. The Sun is much larger than the Earth (shown to scale above) and has a surface temperature of 10,000°F (5,700°C).

**R**ooftop water heaters use tubes to soak up the Sun's heat. The heat energy is then transferred to water pipes. The hot water used by a single household can be supplied by tubes measuring just 22 square feet (two square metres).

Another way to use the Sun's heat is to concentrate the light. At Odeillo, France, a huge wall of mirrors reflects sunlight into a tower-mounted furnace, where temperatures reach up to 6,872°F (3,800°C).

▲ In a rooftop water-heating system, the Sun's rays (1) heat up tubes (2). Heat passes along the tubes to warm cold water (blue arrow) passing through a pipe (3). Hot water (red arrow) can now be used for bathing and laundry.

▲ The research station at Odeillo, France, has 9,500 mirrors mounted on panels. The mirrors reflect the Sun's rays into a furnace in the concrete tower.

# TROUGHS, TOWERS, AND DISHES

Furnaces such as Odeillo are called Concentrating Solar Power (CSP) systems. There are various designs, but they all create heat by concentrating the Sun's rays into a tiny area.

Odeillo is a research station, but there are several CSPs, such as in the sunny Mojave Desert in the United States, that supply power to homes and factories. All CSPs use heat to make steam. The steam then spins turbines to generate electricity.

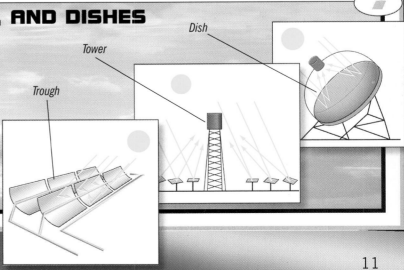

Dish

Tower

Trough

# SOLAR ELECTRICITY

**S**unlight can also be used to make power. Photovoltaic (PV) systems use materials that change the energy in the Sun's rays into electricity, with no need for any other fuel.

**S**olar cells convert sunlight to electricity. Each solar cell provides only a small amount of power, so they are linked together to make a bigger panel. They can be used where electricity from power plants is not available. Space satellites, pocket calculators, water pumps, and parking meters are also sometimes solar powered.

*Pod holds pilot and batteries*

▲ Solar energy can be used in places far away from power lines. This panel supplies a log cabin deep in a forest.

▼ This radio is a design from the 1990s. It has a solar panel on top for power. At night or on cloudy days, a hand-winding generator powers the battery.

▲ *Solar Impulse* is a plane designed to fly around the world, using only solar energy as fuel. It flies up to 39,370 feet (12,000 m) higher than many jetliners.

*Solar panel*

*Pull-out handle for generator*

**E**fficiency is the key to the successful harnessing of solar power. Efficiency is measured by how much of the Sun's energy can be changed to usable power. Most older solar panels have about ten percent efficiency. This means that they can convert about ten percent of the Sun's power into electricity. Newer solar panels have more than 30 percent efficiency.

# SOLAR WINGS AND WHEELS

Solar cells produce electricity during daytime. They can also charge a set of batteries. This is how the designers of the *Solar Impulse* plane hope that it will fly at night. Toward sunset, the pilot will check that the batteries are topped up, ready to replace PV power in the dark.

There have been several successful solar planes. In 1981, the American-built *Solar Challenger* flew from France to England, a 163-mile (262-km) flight.

As well as aircraft, there are also experimental solar cars, and races to test them. The longest solar race is the World Solar Challenge in Australia. It is over 1,864 miles (3,000 km) long.

The first World Solar Challenge, held in 1987, was won by a U.S. car, the GM *Sunraycer*. It covered the course at an average speed of 42 miles per hour (67 km/h). In 2005, the *Nuna 3*, a Dutch car, won the race with an average speed of 64 miles per hour (103 km/h).

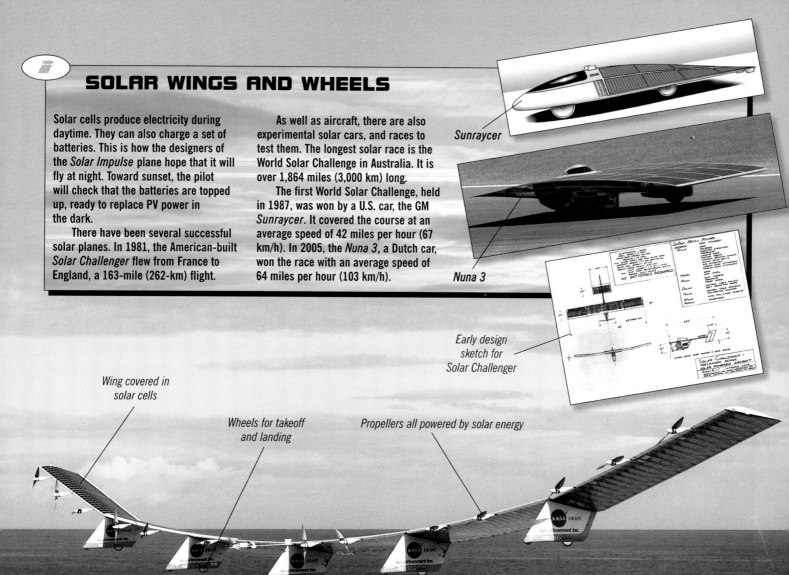

*Sunraycer*

*Nuna 3*

Early design sketch for *Solar Challenger*

Wing covered in solar cells

Wheels for takeoff and landing

Propellers all powered by solar energy

▲ This experimental solar plane had more than 60,000 solar cells that supplied electricity for very high flights.

▼ Solar panels can be placed wherever there is room. These structures all get electricity from sunlight.

There are no greenhouse gases or pollution to worry about with solar, or photovoltaic, panels. The photovoltaic industry is expanding very fast. Photovoltaic panels are getting cheaper and more efficient. In recent years, worldwide sales of PV rooftop panels has increased dramatically, and there are no signs of a slowdown.

# WIND TURBINES

**M**achines that use the power of the wind date back for centuries. Today's wind machines are called wind turbines, or aerogenerators.

▲ Windmills like this were common in Europe for hundreds of years. They were used mostly for grinding wheat to make flour.

**T**here are thousands of wind turbines across the world today. The most common have three long wing-like blades, mounted on a tall tower. The blades meet at a pod called the nacelle. Inside the nacelle is a gearbox and machinery for generating electricity.

► Looking like giant birds of prey, wind turbine blades are stored at the dock before being carried out to sea by assembly ships.

**C**omputer-controlled motors in the nacelle swing the system from side to side, so that the blades face directly into the wind for maximum efficiency. Tall towers are a standard design feature because the wind is usually stronger and steadier high above ground level. Wind turbines are built to stand alone, in small groups, or in large "wind farms," with 50 or more turbines clustered together.

*A 747 jetliner and Enercon E66 wind turbine shown to scale. In real life, the 747 would not fly so close!*

## TWO AIR GIANTS

Modern wind turbines are BIG! This Enercon E66 has a tower more than 262 feet (80 meters) tall, with blades as large as a jetliner's wings. The Enercon E66 has an observation deck at the top. There are more than 300 steps up to the observation deck.

Inside, it is like being in a machine that is almost alive, with noises that range from the regular sighing of the whirling rotor blades, to the soft humming of the wind against the smooth sides of the tower. The view from the top is fantastic!

► The observation deck is no place to visit if you do not like heights.

The world's largest off-shore wind farm is in the North Sea, at Horns Reef, nine miles (14 km) off the coast of Denmark. Advantages in building the turbine here are that winds are stronger at sea, and the 80 turbines do not take up valuable land space. As well, there is no one to complain about the noise the turbines make when they spin.

In December 2002, Horns Reef supplied power for 150,000 homes. Today, four percent of Denmark's electricity comes from the wind.

► Final adjustments are made to a Horns Reef wind turbine.

# NUCLEAR POWER

**T**he power of the atom has been used to make electricity since the 1950s. Atoms are tiny bits of matter that are split to release energy.

▲ Unlike the explosion of a nuclear weapon, a power station uses steady heat to make steam. The steam spins turbines that produce electricity.

**N**uclear power currently provides about one-sixth of the world's electricity. It is not a new technology. The first power-producing nuclear power plant went into service in 1954, in Russia. Today there are more than 440 nuclear power stations around the world.

Nuclear power has a lot of advantages. It is reliable, and does not require fossil fuels, so there are few greenhouse gas emissions.

**T**he waste created from nuclear power is radioactive, or releases **radiation**. Storing radioactive waste is a problem. There may be leaks, even when deadly wastes are sealed in concrete or glass blocks. Accidents at nuclear power plants are also a serious danger. A nuclear explosion occurred at Chernobyl, in Ukraine, which blew out clouds of radioactive material. This happened in 1986, but it is still too dangerous to live there today because of the radiation.

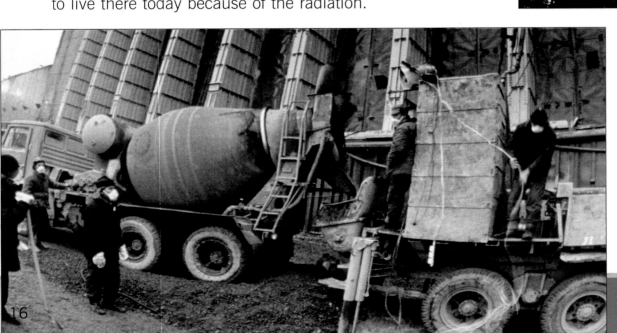

◄ An enormous concrete box was built to seal in the radioactive waste at Chernobyl. Thirty people were killed in the explosion and more than 135,000 were evacuated.

◀ Nuclear power plants produce electricity in large amounts and, despite many people's fears, are reliable sources of energy. The big tower is used to cool water, while radioactive materials are kept safely in the round containment unit.

*Thick concrete is used to safely contain radioactive materials*

## SPLITTING ATOMS

There are different nuclear power plant designs but they all use fission, or heat that is created by splitting atoms.

The reactor is at the heart of the fission system, where atoms of a fuel, such as uranium, are split and controlled. As the uranium atoms break up they release energy and heat. This heat is used to turn water into steam, which then drives generators to make electricity.

Buildings that house nuclear reactors are protected by thick concrete.

The waste from uranium is radioactive. It gives off deadly rays that destroy living things. The nuclear waste created today will remain dangerous for thousands of years. Many scientists opposed to nuclear power argue that storing the waste safely for that long will be impossible.

*Robot arms and other automated equipment handle radioactive materials*

With global warming a big issue, it is likely that new nuclear plants will be built. Many people believe the danger involved in disposing of nuclear waste is not worth it. Today's nuclear waste will not be safe for thousands of years. So, scientists are working on creating cleaner nuclear power systems and safer nuclear waste disposal for the future.

# GEOTHERMAL ENERGY

**D**eep inside the Earth, temperatures reach thousands of degrees. This heat powers volcanoes, but also gives us huge amounts of clean energy.

**G**eothermal energy comes from far below the Earth's cool, rocky crust. Heat is brought to the surface when **groundwater** seeps deep enough to become trapped in hot-rock areas. The water boils and escapes back to the surface as high-pressure steam. By drilling a well in the right place, the steam is trapped and used to drive turbines for electricity.

▲ Scorching hot lava pours from volcanoes. The same heat that causes lava to form can also be used to create electricity.

▼ Steam billows from the geothermal power station at Svartsengi, Iceland. Waste water forms a warm lake for people to swim in (arrow). The water seeps slowly into the ground, to be heated again one day.

Sometimes, temperatures are only high enough for hot water instead of steam. The hot water is still useful for heating homes or for warming greenhouses. Geothermal energy is not one of the biggest energy sources, but it is used in 21 countries around the world, including Iceland, New Zealand, and the U.S. About 60 million people get their electricity from geothermal energy.

▲ The first geothermal experiments were carried out at Larderello, Italy, in 1904, when power was made for five lightbulbs. Today steam from this area supplies power to a million households.

Steam and hot water are not the only ways to use the Earth for energy. The upper ten feet (three meters) of the Earth's surface keeps a nearly constant temperature, between 40°F and 45°F (4°C and 7°C). The ground is usually cooler than the air in summer, but warmer in winter. A **heat pump** uses a system of underground pipes to heat a home. Water is pumped through the pipes, soaking up warmth from the ground for winter heating.

▲ Pipes at New Zealand's Wairakei power station collect and direct steam. Steam blows through the turbine generators at more than 125 miles per hour (200 km/h).

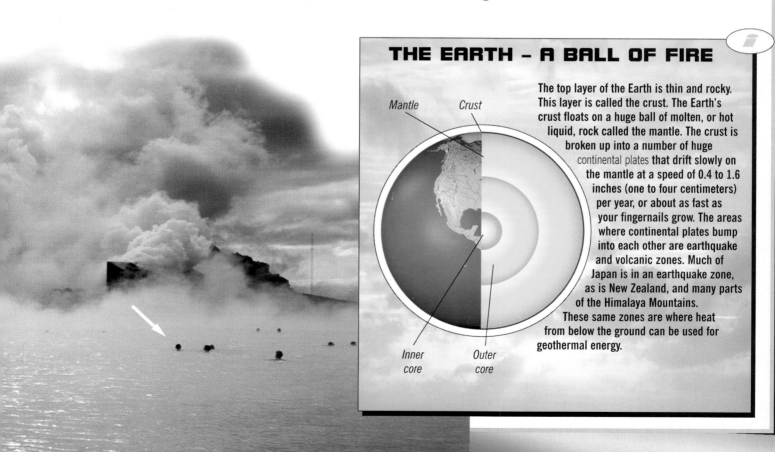

## THE EARTH – A BALL OF FIRE

Mantle    Crust

Inner core    Outer core

The top layer of the Earth is thin and rocky. This layer is called the crust. The Earth's crust floats on a huge ball of molten, or hot liquid, rock called the mantle. The crust is broken up into a number of huge continental plates that drift slowly on the mantle at a speed of 0.4 to 1.6 inches (one to four centimeters) per year, or about as fast as your fingernails grow. The areas where continental plates bump into each other are earthquake and volcanic zones. Much of Japan is in an earthquake zone, as is New Zealand, and many parts of the Himalaya Mountains. These same zones are where heat from below the ground can be used for geothermal energy.

# BIOFUELS

**B**iofuels are made from biomass, or plants and the waste remains of animals. Biomass is burned to create energy, or it is turned into gas or liquid fuels.

Bright yellow Canola is a type of rapeseed

Sorghum waste is used to make insulation and packaging materials

▲ Rapeseed is used across the world for animal feed and cooking oil. It is also used as biofuel for diesel engines.

**W**ood, the oldest renewable energy source of all, is a biofuel. When burned in an open fire, much of the heat from wood is lost. Today, new efficient, high-tech heating systems decrease that waste.

Many different kinds of materials can be used for burning. In some power stations, fast-growing willow trees are burned as fuel. Straw left in the fields after harvest can be used in the same way. Plants and animal waste, such as chicken droppings and cow manure, are also turned into biogases.

▲ The cereal crop sorghum can also be used as a biofuel. This harvester picks out leaves and flowers, and separates the stems. The stems are used to make ethanol, a very clean alcohol fuel that is usually mixed with gasoline.

▼ Animals account for about 17 percent of waste methane gas. A cow produces 160 gallons (600 L) every day!

▲ This biofuel system uses woodchips to fuel a heater. The chips are waste material left over from logging.

**M**achines called digesters are being created to use household waste to make biogas. Biogas is a mixture of methane and carbon dioxide that comes from decomposing, or rotting, waste. Instead of paper and food waste going to a dump, it will be put into the household digester and made into biogas to fuel a heating system or a small electricity generator.

## BURYING THE CARBON

Biofuels burn cleanly and do not add extra greenhouse gases to the environment. Plants have already taken carbon dioxide from the atmosphere while growing, so burning the dead plants does not add any more.

There are ways to reduce carbon emissions from fossil fuels, too. The diagram here shows one method, which buries carbon deep underground in a process called carbon capture.

Natural gas is brought ashore from a drilling rig (1). Special equipment (2) separates the gas into hydrogen and carbon dioxide. The hydrogen is used in a clean-burning power station (3). The carbon dioxide gas is piped to another rig (4) where it is pumped deep underground. The gas pressure helps flush out extra oil and gas.

▶ Burning hydrogen gas and burying carbon safely under the ground could reduce emissions by about 90 percent.

# CLEANER HIGHWAYS

**C**ars and trucks that burn fossil fuels are among the biggest polluters. Cleaner hybrid and fuel-cell power systems may soon replace them.

**H**ybrid-electric power combines a normal **gasoline** engine with an electric motor and batteries. Hybrid vehicles run at low speed on electric power, only using the gasoline engine for accelerating, or speeding up. Some hybrids also have a regenerative system, which uses energy made while braking, or stopping the car, to help recharge the batteries. Hybrids reduce both pollution and the amount of fuel used.

◄ The Japanese Toyota Prius was the first successful hybrid passenger vehicle. The Prius saves fuel when driven around town because at lower speeds, it runs on a battery-powered electric motor.

*Power control unit*

*Electric motor and generator*

*Gasoline engine. Batteries are stored between the back wheels*

**T**he Orion hybrid bus uses a large electric motor, which is charged continuously by a diesel engine. Orions are much cleaner than traditional buses. Pollution of all kinds are cut, including 95 percent of smelly black diesel smoke.

▲ The electric C5 of 1985 was not successful, mostly because its batteries were not powerful enough for long trips.

◄ This Orion hybrid bus carries people around New York City. Before these buses went into service they were tested for more than 500,000 miles (800,000 km) running 21 hours a day.

▲ The Mercedes-Benz Hygenius of 2005 was the first fuel-cell vehicle able to cover more than 250 miles (400 kilometers) on a single tank of hydrogen.

**F**uel cells change chemicals, such as hydrogen and oxygen, into water. In the process, they produce electricity. Unlike a battery, which eventually dies unless recharged, a fuel cell keeps making electricity as long as the chemicals keep flowing through it.

▲ Fuel cells are stored under the floor.

Fuel cells are clean and quiet. New research into improving their performance means that it is likely they will become popular for city driving.

## LIGHT WEIGHT AND ELECTRIC POWER

The General Motors Autonomy concept vehicle uses several ideas to help make driving a little greener.

Its most important feature is a lightweight, flat base named the skateboard. A fuel-cell power supply is fitted into the base, as are the wheels, each with its own electric motor fixed into the hub. The skateboard can be used as a base for different styles of vehicles, such as sports cars or SUVs. The plans call for each one-piece body to simply be dropped onto a skateboard and bolted in place.

These ideas could help future vehicles become cheaper to make, cheaper to run, and greener than current models.

Skateboard base unit

Drop-on one-piece body

# SAVING ENERGY

**A**iming for a green future means more than just using clean or renewable fuels. Finding ways to use less energy is equally as important.

▲ Solar panels and wind turbines help power a supermarket's lighting at night.

**S**aving energy has many benefits, especially where fossil fuels are concerned. Using less fossil fuels reduces pollution and greenhouse gases, and causes fossil fuel supplies to last longer. Lower heat and lighting bills means homeowners save money. There are many ways to "go green," from using low-energy light bulbs to driving shorter distances.

▶ This high-tech home is designed for saving energy. Most of its heating and cooling comes from the heat pump system.

▲ Energy saving ideas include double-glazed windows that keep houses warm in winter.

▲ Poundbury's planners linked a traditional village layout with high-tech building methods. People can go to stores, homes, and offices without wasting energy on cars, cabs, or buses.

**T**own planning is another way to go green. The new village of Poundbury, in England, is built to look like traditional buildings in the area. High-tech materials give Poundbury's houses good insulation that lowers heating costs. The street layout is important, too. Vehicles are allowed in the village, but the narrow, winding streets make it easier for residents to walk or cycle.

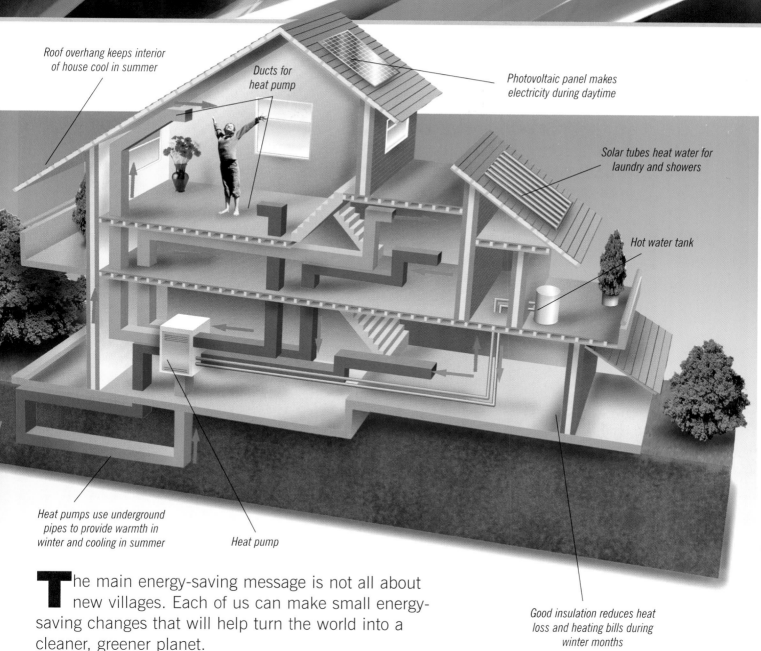

Roof overhang keeps interior
of house cool in summer

Ducts for
heat pump

Photovoltaic panel makes
electricity during daytime

Solar tubes heat water for
laundry and showers

Hot water tank

Heat pumps use underground
pipes to provide warmth in
winter and cooling in summer

Heat pump

Good insulation reduces heat
loss and heating bills during
winter months

The main energy-saving message is not all about new villages. Each of us can make small energy-saving changes that will help turn the world into a cleaner, greener planet.

## CAN WE MAKE CLEAN COAL?

Coal is a fossil fuel that was once widely used for home heating. In many places, clean air laws have made coal-fired furnaces more rare.

Coal is still widely used as a fuel to generate electricity in power stations and it will become even more important as supplies of oil and gas run low.

Some countries use huge amounts of coal. Australia, China, and India make most of their electricity with coal.

There are ways to clean coal and make it burn more efficiently. Coal can be smashed into tiny grains.

The dusty grains burn cleaner. Coal can also be partly burned, in a process that produces syngas, a clean gas suitable for power stations.

Another way to clean coal is to convert it to gas underground. An entire coal seam, or layer, is mixed with oxygen and steam to make the clean-burning gases, methane and hydrogen.

The best way to store waste greenhouse gases from burning coal is to bury them deep underground, using carbon-capture technology.

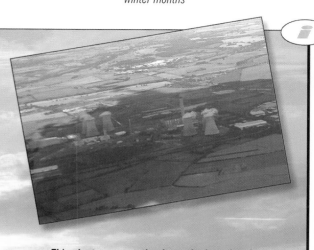

▲ This giant power station burns both coal and gas.

# COMING SOON?

**N**ew, or alternative energy will help us conserve energy, make cleaner fuel, and travel in vehicles that pollute less. Hopefully, pollution and greenhouse gases will become worries of the past.

**S**olar power will be a top green power source of the future. One thing we can do already is place photovoltaic panels on roofs, supplying buildings with free energy from the Sun. In years to come, all new buildings, including homes, can be fitted with solar energy devices, just as they now have water pipes and telephone cables.

◀ The Sunflower 250 is a small electricity generator. It has rows of moving mirrors that focus sunlight onto a photovoltaic panel in the arm at the top.

Turbines mounted in central tower          Greenhouse collector zone

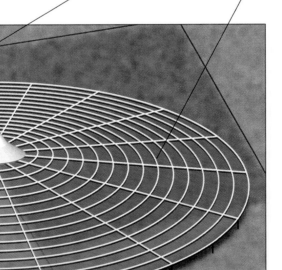

◀ The first big Power Tower is planned for Australia. It is based on a tower system, built in 1982, that ran successfully in Spain for seven years.

**T**he Power Tower links solar and wind energy. It is a simple idea that has been tested in Spain. The Sun heats air under a huge greenhouse. The hot air rises through a hollow central tower, spinning turbines as it soars up. The system makes electricity at night too, because the warmed soil continues to heat air above it.

▲ Photovoltaic plastic tape provides power anywhere that there is light.

The future of nuclear power could lie with huge machines like the International Thermonuclear Experimental Reactor (ITER), being built in France. ITER uses fusion to join atoms together, giving off heat in the process.

There are big advantages if ITER proves that fusion works well. Scientists believe that ITER will produce less radioactive waste and that the waste it does create will not be as dangerous as nuclear waste. ITER's fuel is made from seawater, a resource that is in great supply.

▲ Inside a fusion machine. The power is off at left, and on at right.

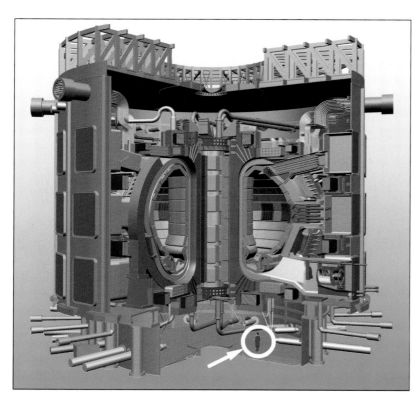

▲ ITER will be a huge machine. Spot the figure in the circle, shown to scale.

## CAN WE ALL HELP?

About 80 percent of the world's energy today comes from fossil fuels. This means that nearly 27.5 billion tons (25 billion tonnes) of carbon dioxide gas goes into the atmosphere. Any attempt to lessen this would have a positive effect on the environment. There are many cleaner energy sources that will be in use in the near future, so environmentalists are hoping that things will improve.

Green power makes sense to reduce pollution and take better care of the planet. We can all do something to help. The easiest way is by saving energy at home. Even little things such as bicycling instead of driving, or turning the furnace down a few degrees, can help. If everyone made energy conservation a habit, it would make a difference.

▼ Riding bicycles and walking are environmentally-friendly methods of travel.

# DISCOVERY TIMELINE

**H**umans have always needed power and heat. In the last few decades, greener power sources have been developed.

▲ Early water mills were used for milling grain, to make flour and other cereal foods. This one is about 250 years old and is still used. Today, the mill's owners sell bags of specially-milled flour.

▲ Antoine Lavoisier, an early pioneer of solar energy, built an experimental furnace to harness the Sun's power.

**500 B.C.** Romans build bath houses with large south-facing windows to let in sunlight for warmth.

**1100s** Windmills are built across Europe. They had been used in ancient Persia as early as 600 B.C.

**1200** First recorded mention of coal mining in Europe.

**1609** Water mills use tidal power at the Bay of Fundy, Canada, home of the world's highest tides.

**1695** French naturalist Georges Buffon (1727-1775) concentrates sunlight using mirrors to set fire to wood and melt lead.

**1700s** Walls are used in Europe to store solar heat for ripening fruit. England and Holland have greenhouses with south-facing glass.

**1712** British inventor Thomas Newcomen (1664-1729), and his partner Thomas Savery (1650-1715) build the first practical steam engine.

**1767** The Swiss naturalist Horace de Saussure builds "hot boxes" that generate enough solar heat to cook eggs placed inside them.

**1769** James Watt is granted a steam engine patent. His first full-scale engines are used in 1776.

**1784** Steam-powered grain mills start replacing traditional windmills.

**1800s** British scientist Michael Faraday (1791-1867) invents the electric motor and generator, and many other devices.

**1827** French engineer Benoit Fourneyron builds the first enclosed water turbine of modern design.

**1839** Welshman William Robert Grove develops the first fuel cell, a device that produces electrical energy by combining hydrogen and oxygen.

**1839** French scientist Edmund Becquerel observes the photovoltaic effect, where some materials produce electric current when exposed to light.

**1857** The first oil well in North America is dug in Oil Springs, Ontario, Canada. In 1859, the first commercial oil well is drilled at Titusville, Pennsylvania.

**1879** U.S. inventor Thomas Edison perfects the first light bulb.

**1882** Thomas Edison's first power station supplies electricity for more than 200 New York homes.

**1882** The world's first hydroelectric power plant goes into operation, on the Fox River, in the United States. A small water wheel powers two generators, giving 25 kW of energy.

**1885** German engineer Karl Benz builds the world's first automobile powered by a gasoline engine.

**1891** U.S. inventor Clarence Kemp patents the first commercial solar water heater.

**1904** Geothermal electricity is produced in Larderello, Italy.

**1920s** Solar water-heating systems, using flat plate collectors, installed in Florida and California homes.

**1941** The first wind turbine to supply a public power system is put into service in Vermont, U.S. It works for four years, until a blade breaks off.

**1950s** Natural gas becomes a popular heating fuel in North America.

**1954** The *New York Times* newspaper forecasts that solar cells will eventually provide limitless access to the Sun's energy.

**1954** First nuclear power plant to produce more than 5,000 kW opens at Obninsk, Russia. Other countries soon open nuclear power plants.

**1958** The U.S. *Vanguard I* satellite is powered by solar cells and operates for eight years.

**1959** Fuel cells are used on many spacecraft, including Moon flights.

**1960** The Geysers geothermal plant opens in California, United States. The first turbine produces 11 megawatts and operates for more than 30 years.

**1966** Rance River tidal power plant opens in France.

**1974** The world's first building heated and powered just by the Sun and wind is built in New Mexico, U.S.

**1986** The Itaipu Dam on the border of Brazil and Paraguay is finished. It is the world's largest hydroelectric dam.

**1990s** Tokyo, Japan, has about 1.5 million buildings with solar water heaters. In Israel, all new buildings have them.

**1991** The first controlled fusion power is produced by a JET research machine, in England. Other fusion projects include a U.S. machine that uses laser beams.

**1995** Geothermal capacity passes 6,000 mW in 20 countries.

**2005** Solar cells are designed to convert 40 percent of the Sun's energy to electricity.

▲ Canada's Bay of Fundy has the world's highest tides, with a 56-foot (17-meter) range between high and low tides. Plans were made to build a tidal barrage across the bay, but there are concerns that this will cause local flooding.

Technician to scale

▲ The Joint European Torus (JET) project was designed to make power by joining atoms together. The next stage is the ITER machine, due to fire up in 2015. If this works as planned, we will have safe fusion power by the year 2025.

# GLOSSARY

► The Sun will continue burning, providing us with power for several billion years.

**A**n explanation of some technical words and concepts used in this book.

**Biomass** The word for all organic, or living or once-living, non-fossil material.

**Continental plate** A vast island of rock containing one of the Earth's continents. The plates float on the Earth's mantle and drift very slowly. The edges of these plates are areas of volcanic and earthquake activity.

**Fossil, fossil fuel** The remains of a plant or animal, found in rock millions of years after its death. Coal, oil, and gas are made of these remains, which is why they are called fossil fuels.

**Fuel cell** A device that converts chemical energy into electricity. Fuel cells typically use hydrogen and oxygen, which make electricity as they combine to form water vapor. Fuel cells are clean, but supplying hydrogen takes energy, so they are not a complete green-power solution.

**Gasoline** A liquid fuel used by most highway vehicles. It is made from crude oil, which comes out of the ground as a thick, black substance that can be refined to produce a wide range of materials, including plastics and synthetic rubber.

**Generator** A machine that converts rotary, or spinning, motion into electrical energy. The spinning motion is usually supplied by turbines which are driven by steam or water.

**Global warming** The effect of too many human-produced greenhouse gases in the atmosphere, raising temperatures higher than normal.

**Gravity** The force that attracts objects toward the center of the Earth. Gravity helps create tides.

**Greenhouse effect** The blanketing effect of the atmosphere, which traps heat, making the Earth warmer and allowing it to sustain life.

**Greenhouse gases** The gases that trap heat close to the Earth's surface. These include water vapor and carbon dioxide. Burning fossil fuels adds carbon dioxide to the atmosphere.

**Groundwater** Water flowing within porous rock, after it has seeped below the ground. Water flows back to the surface at natural springs and swamps. It is also brought to the surface by drilling wells.

**Heat pump** A machine for home heating. It has pipes filled with liquid buried in the soil outside the home. In winter, the liquid takes in heat from the soil. In summer, when the soil is cooler than the air, the same liquid becomes a coolant.

**Hydrogen** The lightest and most abundant gas. Hydrogen burns cleanly and, when combined with oxygen, forms water. It is used in fuel cells.

**Ice cap** The permanent areas of ice at the North and South Poles. Ice at the North Pole floats on the Arctic Ocean. Ice at the South Pole lies over the continent of Antarctica.

**Pollution** The ways in which the environment is harmed, or dirtied, by substances such as industrial waste and exhaust gases.

**Radiation** Natural wave energy, such as radio waves and light rays. Some materials, such as plutonium and uranium, which are used at nuclear power stations, give off radioactive rays that can damage living cells. Too much radiation causes sickness or death.

**Renewable** Fuels that do not run out as they are used. They include wind, hydro, tidal, solar, and biomass.

**Reservoir** A natural or human-made lake. Reservoirs are often used to control the amount of water that goes through a dam.

**Rig** The name for an oil or gas drilling platform. Rigs may be built on land or offshore, in shallow seas.

**Solar cell** A flat piece of material that converts sunlight to electricity. The process is called the photovoltaic (PV) effect. Most solar cells are made of silicon.

**Tides** The rising and falling of water levels in the ocean due to the gravitational forces of the moon and the Sun. Ocean shores experience high and low tides twice each day.

**Watt (W)** A unit of power, named after the Scottish engineer James Watt (1736-1819), to honor his pioneering work with steam engines.

▲ Power lines are an important part of the electricity system. They carry power from where it is generated to where it is needed.

# GOING FURTHER

The Internet is a good way to keep up with the latest on alternative energy and green power. These addresses are useful general-interest sites, which can lead you to more detailed sources.

http://www.nasa.gov
The homepage of the space agency NASA. It has a lot of information about our planet.

http://www.bp.com/home.do?categoryId=1
The site of one of the big oil companies, with information on what they are doing about green power solutions.

http://www.foei.org/
The international homepage of Friends of the Earth, one of the biggest environmental groups. The site includes information about the environment.

http://www.nei.org/
This site promotes the postive aspects of the nuclear industry.

http://www.eere.energy.gov/RE/solar.html
A site of the U.S. Department of Energy that has useful information about solar power, as well plenty of links.

http://journeytoforever.org/biofuel.html
A fun site about making biofuels.

If you want more green power information, then do not forget to use your school or local library. There are also many museums and exhibitions about energy.

# INDEX

Acknowledgements
We wish to thank all those individuals and organizations that have helped to create this publication. Information and images were supplied by:
Steve Allen, Martin Bond, Tony Bostrom, BAe Systems, BP Plc, Tony Craddock, Daimler Chrysler Corp., Bernhard Edmaier, EFDA-JET, Energy Innovations Inc., Enviromission Ltd., Tommaso Guicciardini, David Jefferis, MCT Seagen, NASA Space Agency, Novosti, NREL, Gavin Page, General Motors Corp, Konarka Technologies Inc., David Parker, Science Photo Library, Solar Impulse/EPFL-Artist Claudio Leonardi, Toyota Motor Corp., Vestas Wind Systems S/A Denmark, Wavegen